© Rod Campbell 1988
First published 1988 by
Campbell Blackie Books
7 Leicester Place · London WC2H 7BP

ISBN 1 85292 016 5

Printed in Singapore

Little Learners

shapes

Rod Campbell

CAMPBELL BLACKIE BOOKS

square

A square has four corners
and four sides the same size.

Here are some square shapes –

this book

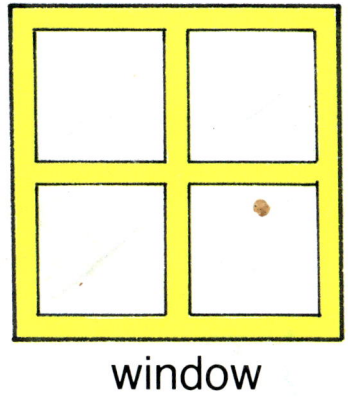

window

sugar lumps

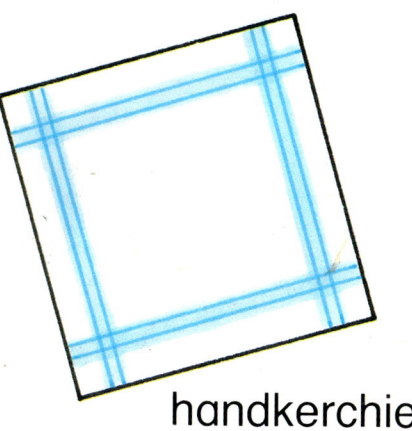

handkerchief

building bricks

jack-in-the-box

rectangle

A rectangle has four corners.
It is like a stretched square!

Here are some rectangle shapes –

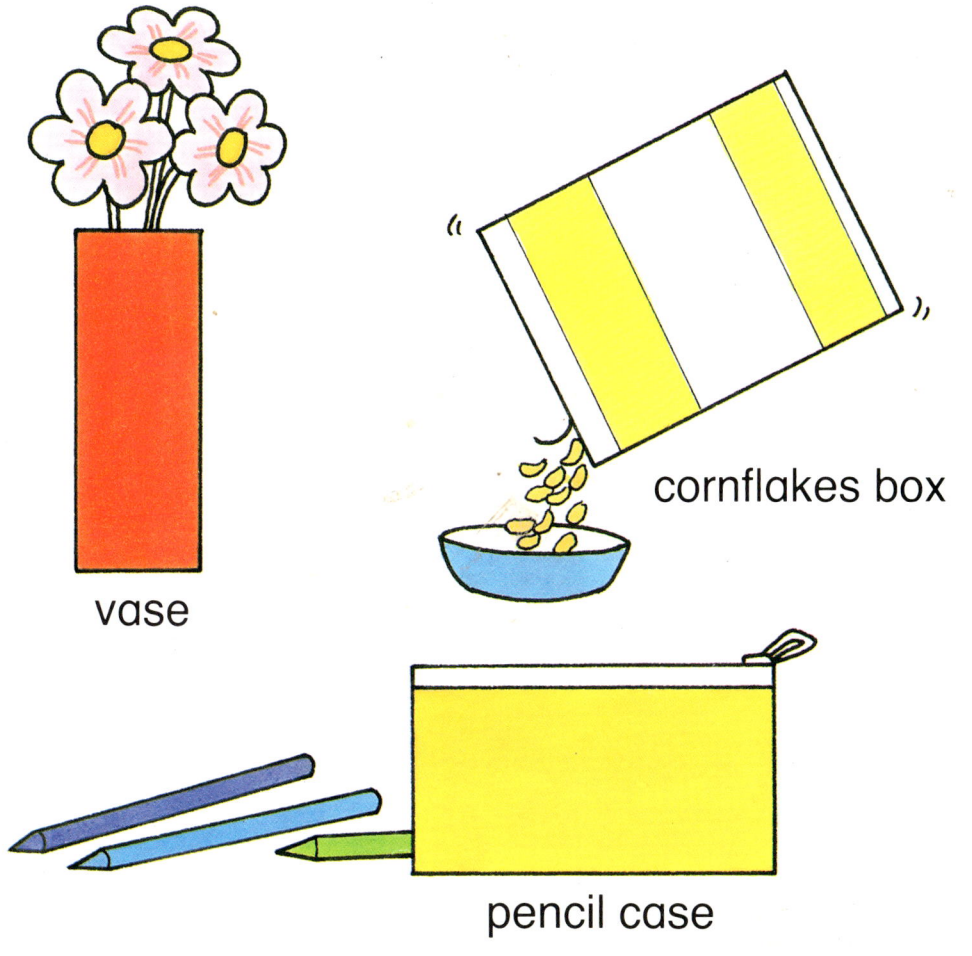

vase

cornflakes box

pencil case

letter

To/ The Queen
Buckingham Palace,
LONDON.

letter box

stamps

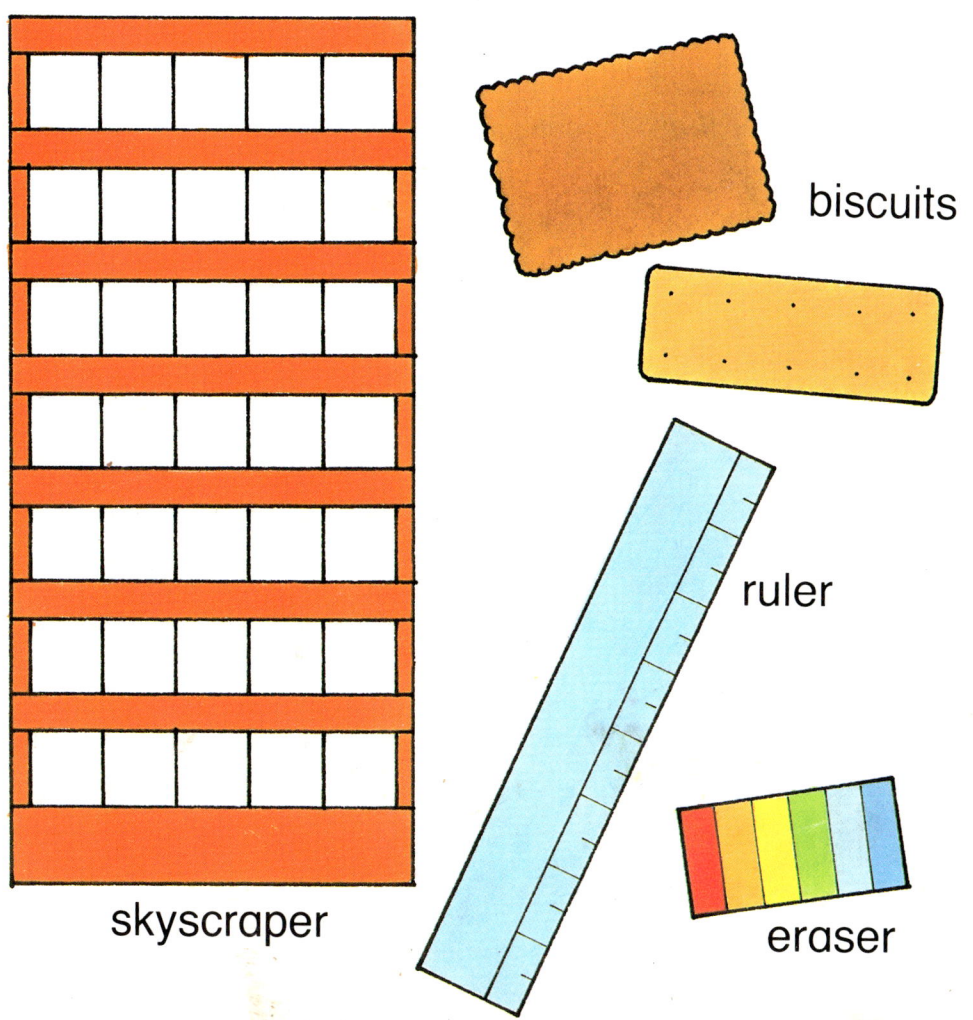

skyscraper

biscuits

ruler

eraser

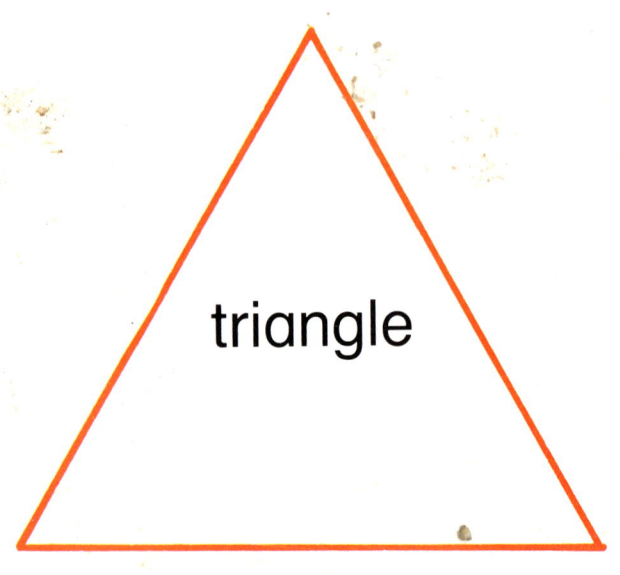

triangle

A triangle has three corners and only three sides.

Here are some triangle shapes –

cheese

magician's hat

ice-cream cone

flag

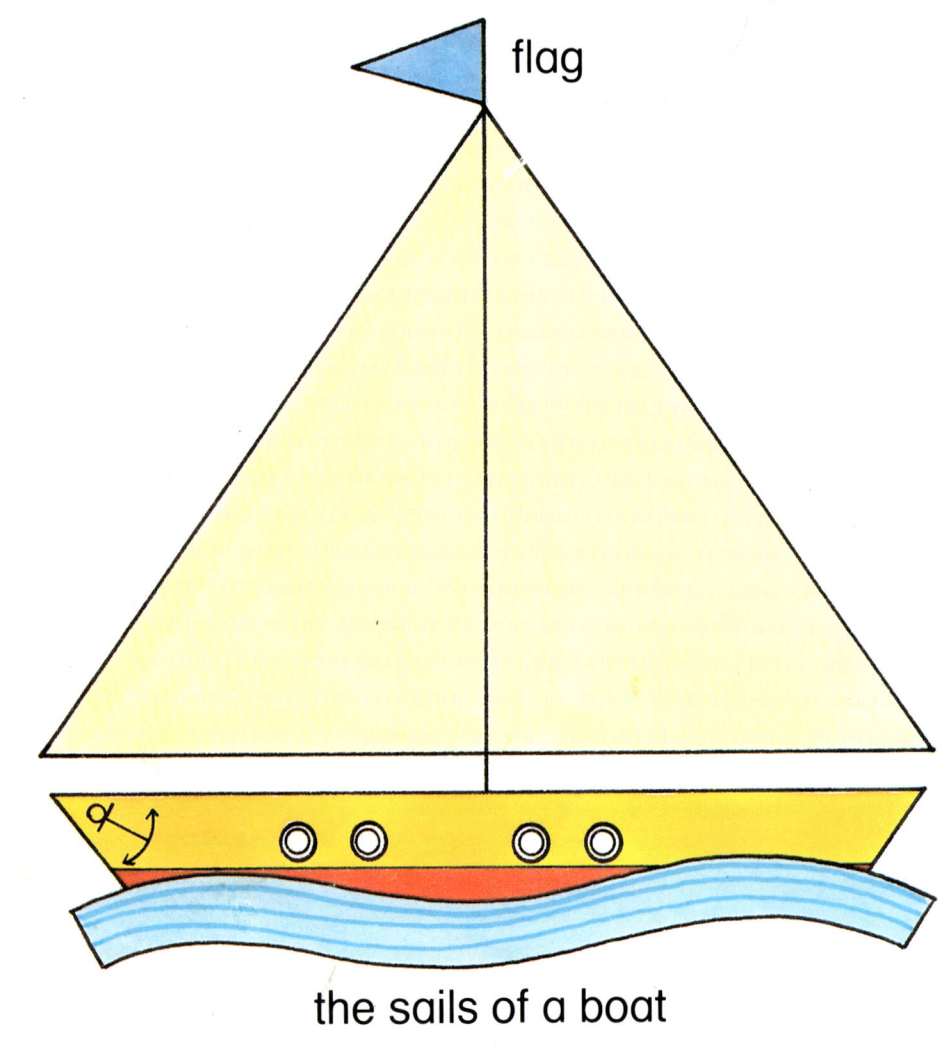

flag

the sails of a boat

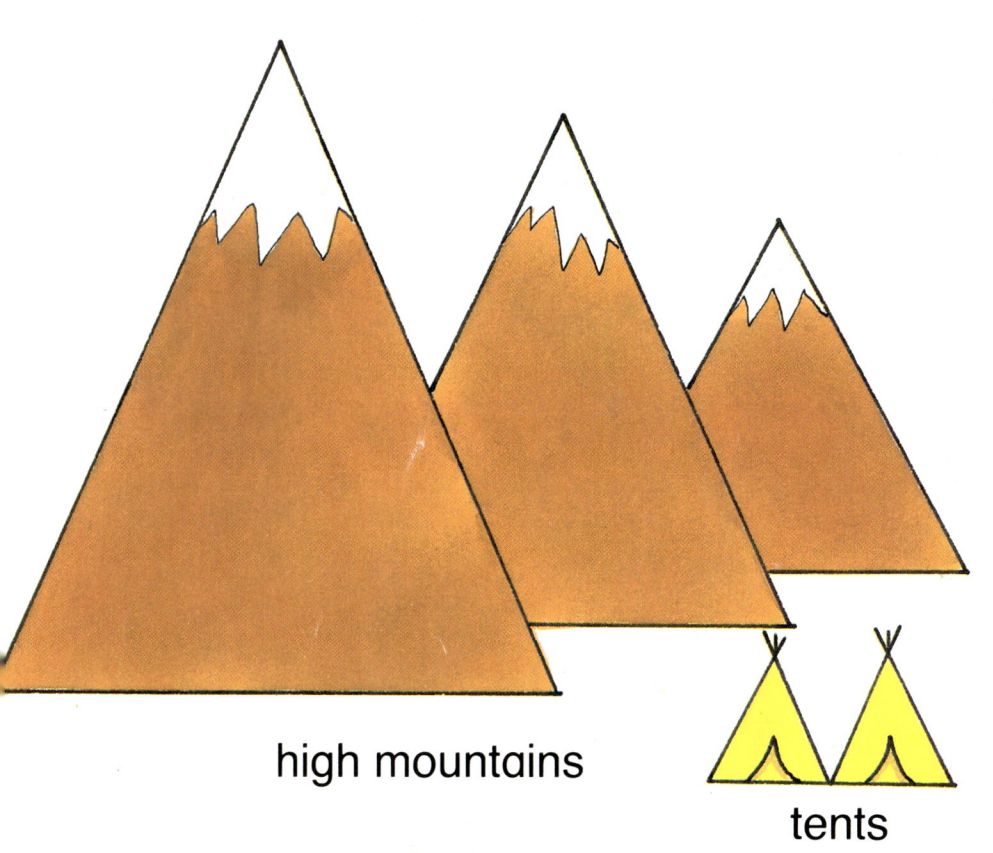

high mountains

tents

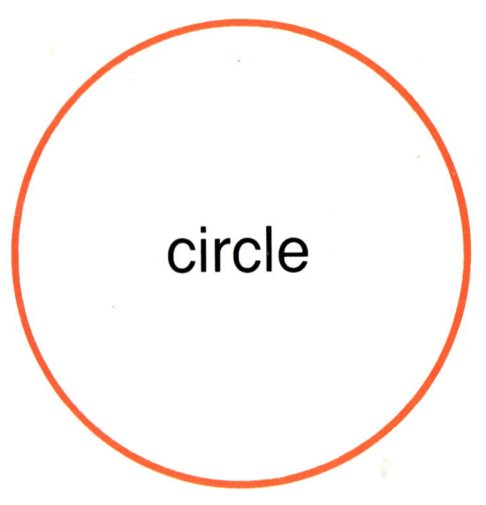

circle

A circle has no corners.
It is completely round.

Here are some circle shapes –

sun

moon

orange

bicycle wheels

tomato

counters

buttons

clock

semicircle

A semicircle is a circle
which has been cut in half.

Here are some semicircle shapes –

piece of lemon

the setting sun

hat

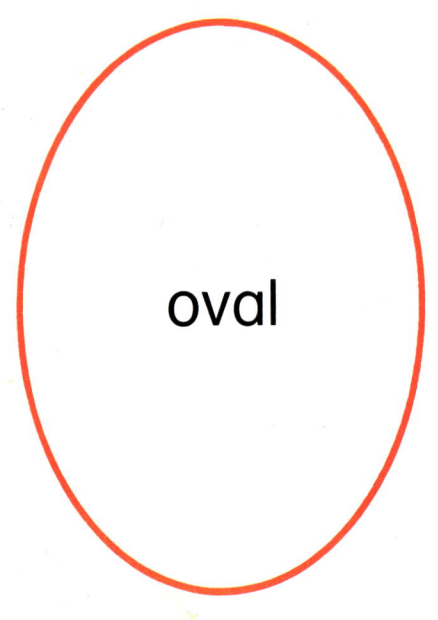

oval

An oval is like a squashed circle!

Here are some oval shapes –

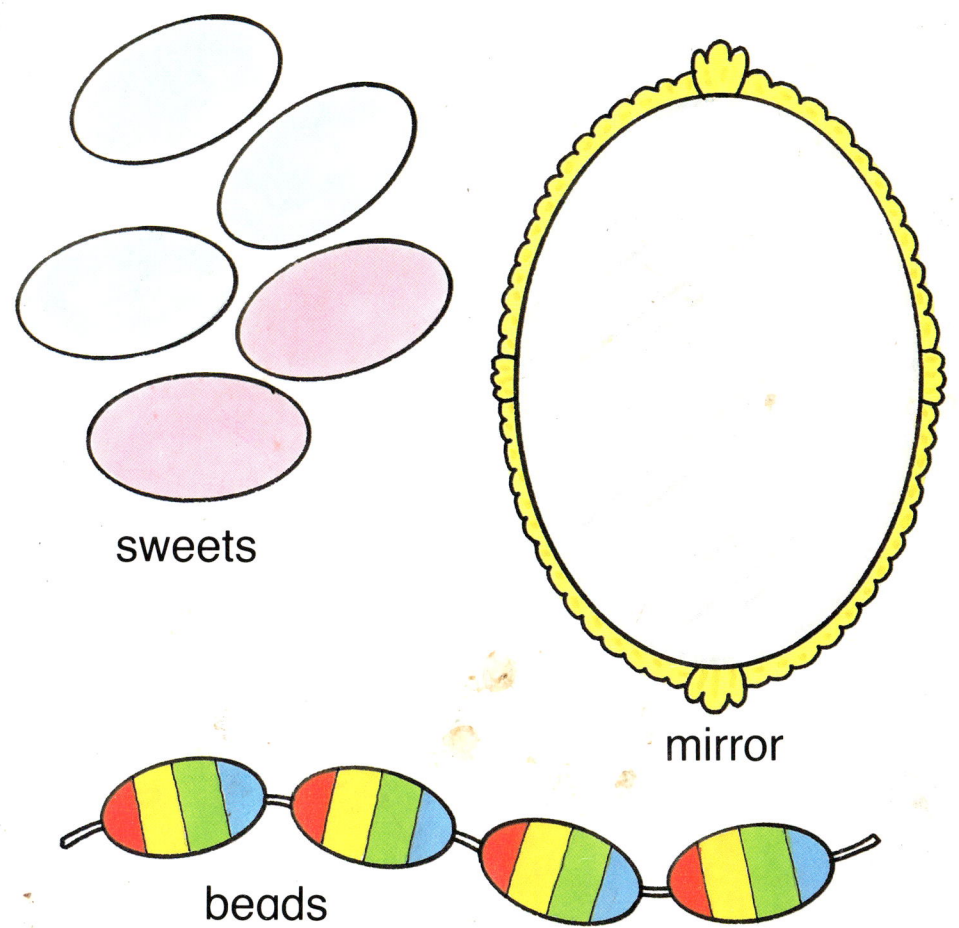

sweets

mirror

beads

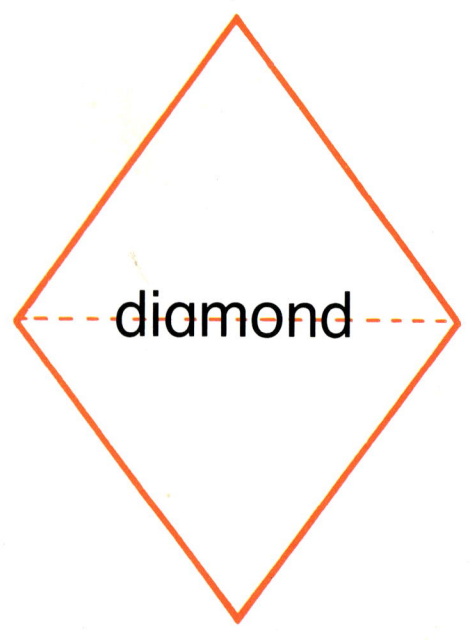

diamond

A diamond is like two triangles joined together.

Here are some diamond shapes –

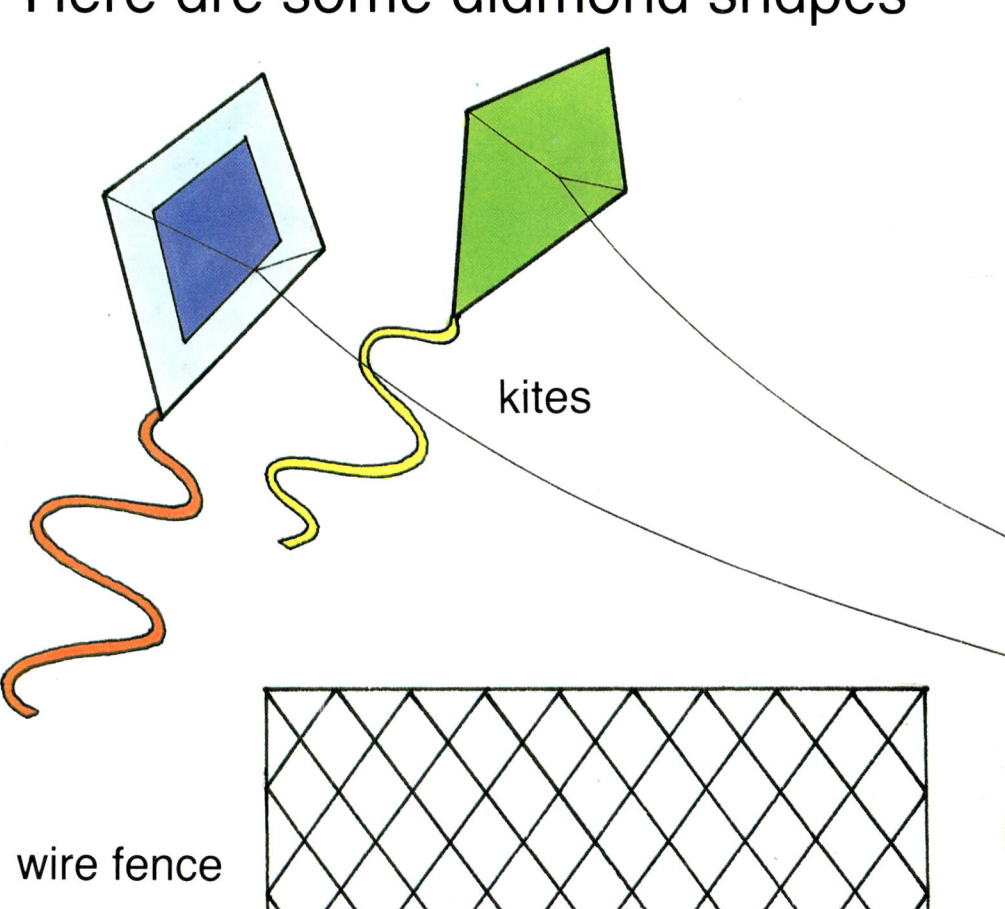

kites

wire fence

What shapes can you see?

sweets

spoon

lollipop

bowl

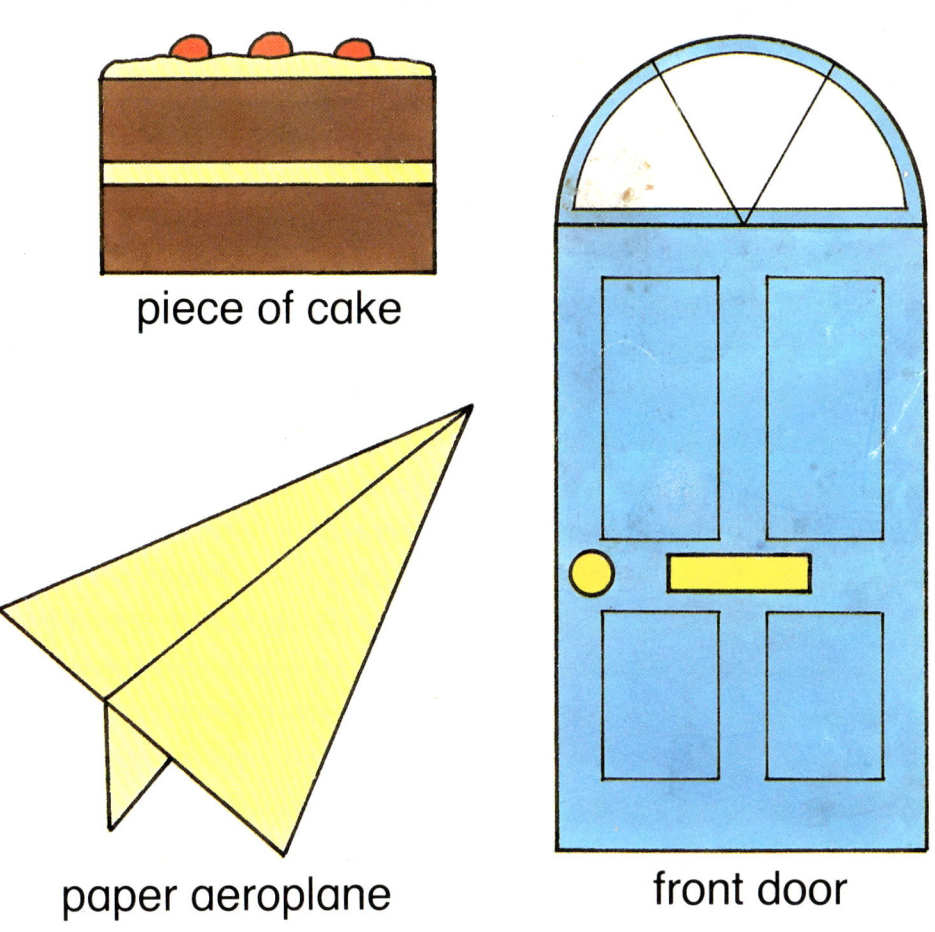

piece of cake

paper aeroplane

front door